04/17

The Scared Elephant

By JENNA LAFFIN

Illustrated by BRIAN HARTLEY

Music Produced by ERIK KOSKINEN and
Recorded at REAL PHONIC STUDIOS

CANTATA
LEARNING

WWW.CANTATALEARNING.COM

CANTATA
LEARNING

Published by Cantata Learning
1710 Roe Crest Drive
North Mankato, MN 56003
www.cantatalearning.com

A note to educators and librarians from the publisher: Cantata Learning has provided the following data to assist in book processing and suggested use of Cantata Learning product.

Publisher's Cataloging-in-Publication Data
Prepared by Librarian Consultant: Ann-Marie Begnaud
Library of Congress Control Number: 2015958185
    The Scared Elephant
    Series: Me, My Friends, My Community : Songs about Emotions
    By Jenna Laffin
    Illustrated by Brian Hartley
    Summary: A song about feeling scared.
    ISBN: 978-1-63290-548-2 (library binding/CD)
    ISBN: 978-1-63290-645-8 (paperback/CD)
Suggested Dewey and Subject Headings:
    Dewey: E 152.4
    LCSH Subject Headings: Emotions – Juvenile literature. | Friendship – Juvenile literature. | Emotions – Songs and music –
Texts. | Friendship – Songs and music – Texts. | Emotions – Juvenile sound recordings. | Friendship – Juvenile sound recordings.
    Sears Subject Headings: Emotions. | Friendship. | School songbooks. | Children's songs. | Folk music.
    BISAC Subject Headings: JUVENILE NONFICTION / Social Topics / Emotions & Feelings. | JUVENILE NONFICTION
/ Music / Songbooks. | JUVENILE NONFICTION / Social Topics / Friendship.

Book design and art direction, Tim Palin Creative
Editorial direction, Flat Sole Studio
Music direction, Elizabeth Draper
Music produced by Erik Koskinen and recorded at Real Phonic Studios

Printed in the United States of America in North Mankato, Minnesota.
072016   0335CGF16

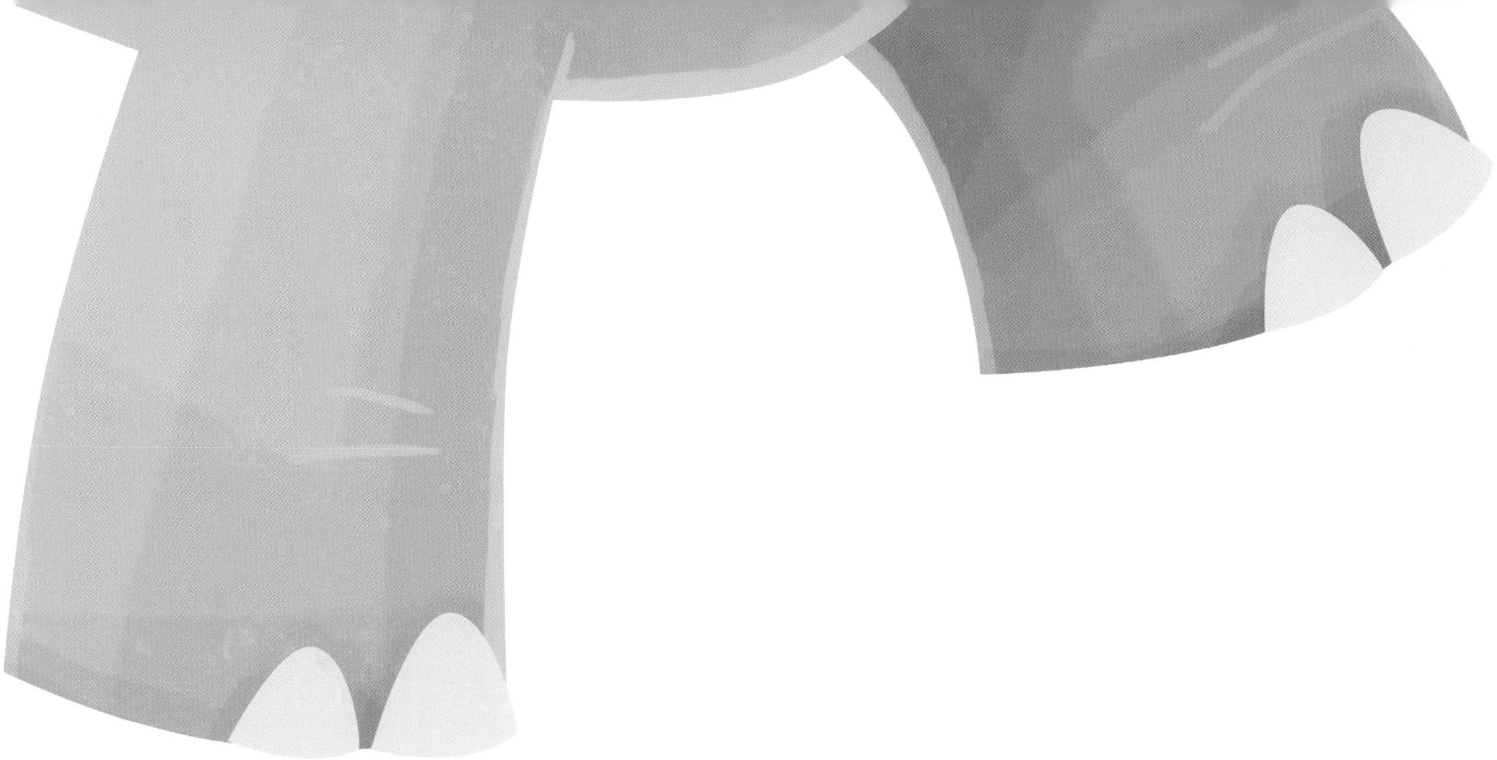

ACCESS THE MUSIC!

SCAN
CODE
WITH
MOBILE
APP

CANTATALEARNING.COM

We all have feelings. We may feel happy, sad, mad, or even scared. Some people are scared of the dark. Others are **frightened** by spiders and snakes. It is okay to be afraid when things scare you.

Turn the page to see how friends help Elephant and Spider overcome their fears. Remember to sing along!

Why are you afraid?
What do you fear?

Be **brave**.
Be brave.

Look around.
Your friends are near.

The Elephant cried,
"I'm scared of Spider,
sitting in the night.

I'm scared he will crawl
and give me a bite!"

Turn on a light.
You'll be just fine.

See? Spider is nice.
He's really quite kind.

Why are you afraid?
What do you fear?

Be brave.

Be brave.

Look around.
Your friends are near.

Then Spider cried,
"I'm scared of Elephant
and his big, big feet!

I'm scared he will **stomp** on me
when he's walking down the street!"

Just say, "Hello"
when Elephant walks by.

Give a friendly smile
because he's really quite **shy**.

Elephant and Spider,
one big, one small,
they both were afraid
for no reason at all!

19

Why are you afraid?
What do you fear?

Be brave.
Be brave.

Look around.
Your friends are near.

The Scared Elephant

Why are you afraid?
What do you fear?
Be brave.
Be brave.
Look around.
Your friends are near.

The Elephant cried,
"I'm scared of Spider,
sitting in the night.
I'm scared he will crawl
and give me a bite!"

Turn on a light.
You'll be just fine.
See? Spider is nice.
He's really quite kind.

Why are you afraid?
What do you fear?
Be brave.
Be brave.
Look around.
Your friends are near.

Then Spider cried,
"I'm scared of Elephant
and his big, big feet!
I'm scared he will stomp on me
when he's walking down the street!"

Just say, "Hello"
when Elephant walks by.
Give a friendly smile
because he's really quite shy.

Elephant and Spider,
one big, one small,
they both were afraid
for no reason at all!

Why are you afraid?
What do you fear?
Be brave.
Be brave.
Look around.
Your friends are near.

The Scared Elephant

Americana
Erik Koskinen

Chorus
Why are you a-fraid? What do you fear? Be brave. Be brave. Look a-round. Your friends are near. The

Verse
1. The El - e-phant cried, "I'm scared of Spi-der, sit-ting in the night. I'm scared he will crawl and give me a bite!"

Pre Chorus
Turn on a light. You'll be just fine. See? Spi - der is nice. he's real - ly quite kind.

Chorus

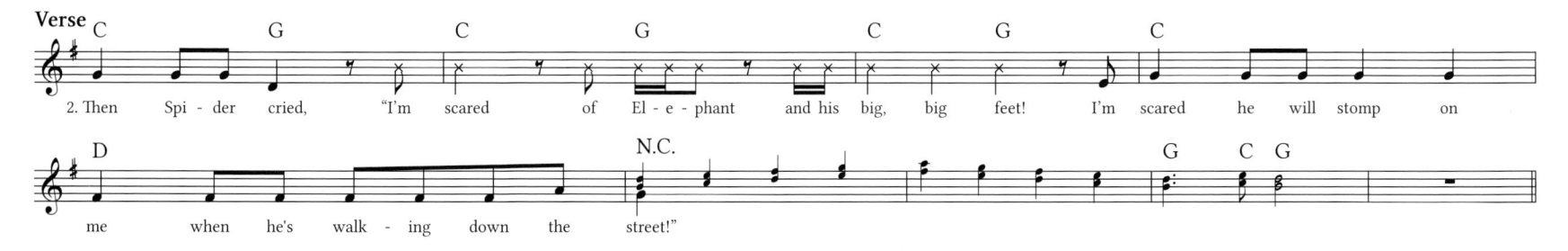

Verse
2. Then Spi - der cried, "I'm scared of El - e - phant and his big, big feet! I'm scared he will stomp on

me when he's walk - ing down the street!"

Pre Chorus
Just say, "Hello"
when Elephant walks by.
Give a friendly smile
because he's really quite shy.

Pre Chorus
Elephant and Spider,
one big, one small,
they both were afraid
for no reason at all!

Chorus

GLOSSARY

brave—feeling or showing no fear

frightened—afraid

shy—afraid to talk to people or to be around them

stomp—to walk with very heavy or noisy steps

GUIDED READING ACTIVITIES

1. Think of a time that you felt scared. What were you scared of? What did you do when you felt afraid?

2. Has someone ever helped you when you were scared? What did they do to make you feel better?

3. Draw a line down the middle of a piece of paper. On one side, draw things that make you feel scared. On the other side, draw things that make you feel happy. You will sometimes be scared, but you will be happy again, too!

TO LEARN MORE

Aboff, Marcie. *Everyone Feels Scared Sometimes*. Minneapolis: Picture Window Books, 2010.

Dahl, Michael. *Cold Feet*. Minneapolis, MN: Picture Window Books, 2011.

Nichols, Cheyenne. *Scared Is…* Mankato, MN: Capstone Press, 2012.

Yarlett, Emma. *Orion and the Dark*. London: Templar Publishing, 2015.